ANATOMY OF YOUR DECISION-MAKING

A PRACTICAL GUIDE FOR
UNDERSTANDING THE IMPACT OF
INFLUENCE ON THE CHOICES WE MAKE

By

Joe Kenley

This book is dedicated to my wife, Rhoda, who believed, encouraged, and supported me through this project since the conception of the idea. This book is also dedicated to my three sons, Justin, Bryce, and River, for giving me a reason to share what I've learned to help them navigate their life journeys with more clarity to hopefully minimize the detours by preparing a path.

ACKNOWLEDGMENTS

Thanks to Creflo Dollar Ministries and Lighthouse Church of Dexter for teaching me how to live a Christ-centered life and to step out of my comfort zone and use my God-given gifts to impact those with whom I come into contact. Thanks to P.O.P Publishing for assisting me through the publishing process for this book. I also want to give a BIG thanks to my content contributors and supporters who pre-ordered *Anatomy of Your Decision-Making: A Practical Guide for Understanding the Impact of Influence on the Choices We Make*

Tanya Blair – VA
www.WEBPBM.com
David Cummings - NJ
Kay Davidson, MO
Gabrielle Decarvalho - FL
Al Forehand – NJ
https://ASCOTECHNOLOGIES.wixsite.com/ascotech nologies
Daniel Higgins - GA
www.WHY1INCOME.com
Tiffany Hill - MD
www.PUZZLEANDBLOOM.com
Shirley Jasper - MD

Tami'ka Jones - PA
www.THEZURIOFNUBIAFASHIONS.com
Kalynn Kendrick - NV   Empire Silver Investment
Group
Ian Lewis - NY
Scott & Amanda Moore - MO
Trina Obi Esq. - NJ
Brandon O'Mara - Canada
www.BRANDONOMARA.com
Damani Peeples - CA -
https://DAMANIPEEPLES.ESPRITA.com/
Robin Sargent Ph.D. - GA
www.IDOLCOURSES.com
Darryl Scipio Esq. - NJ
www.SCIPIOLAW.com
Tanisha H. Shaw - NJ -
www.OPTIMAL-LIVINGMAGAZINE.com
Vanessa Turner - NJ
facebook.com/MSVANESSASTURNER
Michael Wallace - CA
https://www.linkedin.com/in/mike-wallace-b580066
Wilson Wallace - GA
Shamek Weddle - TN
Sharrieff De'Johnette - VA
Russell & Alonda Whiting - VA
Jelani Wilson - VA
https://www.linkedin.com/in/JelaniWilson

CONTENTS

OVERVIEW

Making a decision is something that everyone must encounter in his or her life. Some of the choices we make are simple while others are more complex. "What should I post on Instagram?" "Should I be in this relationship?" "Why do I get angry so quickly?" "Why do I think about things the way I do?" These are some common examples of questions we ask ourselves that will prompt us to do something.

Many times when having to choose between multiple options for the best outcome, it requires us to think about how our choices will affect us or any party or entity that has a stake in it. There are some decisions we make that prompt us to act in similar situations as the result of a learned experience, habit, careful consideration, or even out of fear. One common factor that influences us to make a choice is our motivation towards an outcome. What strengthens or weakens that motivation respectively is our mindset towards the things that are known or what's unknown that will happen between deciding and the outcome. What we also need to be aware of is that motivation is a result of an influence. Influences affect the way we think and feel. With this understanding, we can begin to identify the influences in our lives and reflect on the impact they have on the decisions we make. Whether it is how we respond to confrontation, choosing whether or not to take action or the careers we choose, your influence is the catalyst and should be examined to help navigate us to our desired outcomes.

Through reflection, we uncover the **what, when, why, and how's** for our choices. It will help you recognize the conditions that contribute to your strengths as well as the necessary improvements that need to be made when a choice is required. This book will discuss explanations from psychological theories, genetic and environmental influences, sources of influence, decision-making strategies, indecisiveness, and how our attitudes and beliefs contribute to why we think and choose the way we do.

CHAPTER 1:
DECISIONS! DECISIONS!
DECISIONS!

There is a question that all humans say aloud or think in their minds that is the precursor to what will happen in their lives. The response to this question may be something that shows up immediately or in the distant future. One thing for certain about this question is that it's always personal and there is always a correlated response to it. Responses to this personal question are path setters that lead to a destination we are all eventually headed towards. A path that will not only impact you personally but also the people connected to you.

Do you have an idea what this pivotal question is? It is so simple that it is not a mystery to know but it is also a question so frequently asked that we subconsciously don't consider its weight. With several expressions that can be used in its place, the most frequent question that humans ask is "What am I going to do?" As you can see, this is a short and simple question. This question precedes an action which makes it a point of decision. Decisions are made all the time for anything we encounter that requires us to make a choice. This also includes the choice for our own attitudes. Some decisions are made after careful consideration with or without counsel, while at other times they may be made solely and sporadically. Have you ever considered why some personal decisions are harder than others to make? More than likely, it is because of the possible consequences that would result from the decisions that will be made. So considering the potential outcomes, both beneficial and damaging, we then decide to put an intent into action.

Another question we need to ask ourselves is "Why do I make decisions the way I do?" This specific question will lead to a personal discovery that will identify the path that begins with a source of influence and lead us to how we arrive at the current conditions of our thinking and physical wellbeing.

With these two questions in mind, we'll journey through the processes of our unique decision-making, identify indecisiveness and its effects, review strategies for choosing, and show the process at work through personal stories. Psychological theories related to making a decision will be discussed as well as identifying how spirituality, morals, and people impact our lives and ways of thinking.

CHAPTER 2:
THEORIES

It's not uncommon to wonder why we do things or think the way we do. There are several psychological theories that attempt to explain how we choose. Without sounding like a textbook, I want to share the ideas from a few theories that address decision-making.

The Social Learning Theory is one developed by Albert Bandura which asserts that we learn from observing others by seeing the outcome of their actions. In this theory, through observation, an individual can make a decision if they want to duplicate an act that he/she observed someone else do base on the consequences of the behavior.

Choice Theory developed by William Glasser is another. The concept is that all behavior has a purpose to get what you want. The theory asserts that there are five core concept needs. 1) Survival – What's necessary to sustain life which facilitates safety and security. 2) Love and Belonging – The motivation to be connected to others. 3) Power - The motivation to have significance, to be competent and respected, to achieve goals, and a desire to leave a legacy. 4) Freedom – The desire to be independent and autonomous and have options. The ability to move freely without being restricted. 5) Fun – Encompasses pleasure, humor, play, relaxation, and relevant learning.

Another theory is the Hierarchy of Needs by Abraham Maslow. It is a motivational theory that explains the needs humans have that must be satisfied in order to thrive in the things we do. He identified and illustrated these needs in a diagram shaped like a pyramid that described the order of need fulfillment before a person is self-fulfilled. At the base of the pyramid is 1) Physiological Needs – What we need to survive as humans and includes food, water, and rest. Next is 2) Safety Needs - The need for shelter and a sense of feeling secure. The next is 3) Belongingness and Love Needs - The need for intimate relationships and friends. To build upon the need for connectedness are 4) Esteem Needs - The feeling of accomplishment. The top of the pyramid is 5) Self-Actualization - Achievement of self-fulfillment of one's hopes and ambitions.

When writing this book, I didn't want to just write from my reflection of the decisions I have made or from the stories of how other people made choices that impacted their lives. My desire is to take a critical look at the process of making a decision, to help identify our current position (our present thoughts and biases), the direction we're headed, and to uncover why we decided the path we are taking right now. The theories I chose to include are points of reference to consider the influences that lead to decisions. These psychological theories have a common theme, that individuals have control over their own actions. There may be outside factors that influence a decision but there's something in the inside of all of us that triggers the desire for us to act or to pause.

CHAPTER 3:
METHOD APPLICATION

In my life, like many others, I made decisions that had amazing outcomes but I also made many decisions that were quite the contrary. A great decision I made was to earn a graduate degree in Counseling. This helped me fulfill a desire to motivate people to accomplish their goals, to help people get unstuck in their lives, inspire hope, and help people to live their best life even if current conditions are in opposition. The process for my decision to pursue counseling was not perfectly laid out and planned. It was the result of not being satisfied or feeling fulfilled with what I was doing prior to becoming a counselor. Here's how it began. After I earned my undergraduate degree in Psychology, I got married and needed a job. You may have heard the saying "Happy wife, happy life." I needed to have a consistent income to rent an apartment of our own and survive. So to fulfill that need, I found a job that was doing a mass hiring and was loosely related to my psychology degree. In fact, my fiancé, now wife, found the opportunity before I did. I began working as a telephone sales representative for a growing financial institution. In the beginning, all went well. I earned the consistent income I needed to rent an apartment and have a comfortable home environment for me and my wife.

I excelled in my position within a couple of years. I was promoted from a sales representative to a loan officer and then qualified to work from home based on the volume of my sales transactions. I earned a salary plus commissions and thought I was living on top of the world. I took advantage of the opportunity to work from home and moved to Atlanta, Georgia from Virginia. During my first-year of telecommuting, I enjoyed being able to work from home until my employer decided to change the commission scale which made it more challenging to earn the money I was used to making. I enjoyed helping others so I continued in my position for as long as I was able to hold out even with a decreased income. I tolerated the work but soon became frustrated with the change in my lifestyle resulting from the change in my income. I also became frustrated by the lack of social interaction with people outside the walls of my apartment. I was home for eight or more hours, tied to a headset, talking to a computer screen. I did it to save money to move out of my apartment to purchase a house because I knew my wife and I wanted to own a home.

I was in a new state, missing out on meeting people face-to-face and many times too tired to do anything after work hours. My wife worked outside the home during the day so she was able to meet people and explore Atlanta. She learned the different road routes and found places she wanted to check out. I felt as though I was missing out on everything besides going to the grocery store on the weekends and dinner and a movie from time to time. I spoke with my wife and let her know that I needed change. I wanted to meet and interact with new people, see how people in my community functioned during the workweek, and simply go outside for more time than an assigned lunch break. I decided to apply for a bank manager position at a local branch of my bank. It was my way to get out of the house and meet people. Thankfully, I was hired and transferred from my telecommuting position for the manager position at the local branch.

I found it refreshing to get out of the house more often and to meet new colleagues and customers face-to-face. For almost two years, I was excited to strategize work goals with my team and help customers with their banking needs. I had stories about my daily encounters with my customers and bank crew when talking to my wife after work. I felt connected to my community. I was able to explore new areas in Atlanta during the day when I had meetings with other branch managers and bank administrators. It was exactly what I needed to not feel boxed in until I realized providing bank services really did not interest me anymore. I wanted to utilize my degree in a field more related to my interests. This is when I decided to enroll in graduate school to earn a degree in Counseling.

I enrolled in a program that offered weekend courses because I still needed to work to help support my growing family. Within three years, I earned my degree and switched careers soon after.

My example describes the decisions I made based on the needs I had in my life at the time. Needs that were to benefit my marriage, family, as well as my personal need for social engagement. There were times when it became difficult for me and my family as a result of the decisions I made. It was tough! Even after becoming a counselor, I questioned my decision even though I was happy when helping people. I certainly made more money in the banking system than I made as a community counselor. I realized that something more impactful than money was a motivator for me that made me feel good about what I was doing. Earning a graduate degree and working as a counselor opened doors for me to teach undergraduate college students psychology and counseling courses, then become an academic advisor, work for the federal government as a guidance counselor, and then was hired as a location director for a community college. I enjoy being able to help people get from the starting point where I meet them to where they want to go. Whether it's one-to-one or speaking to a group, sharing helpful information with the expectations that it will give someone the advantage in his or her life is what I like to do.

CHAPTER 4:
THE STRENGTH OF INFLUENCE

When considering any of the psychological theories I mentioned for my decision-making example, you can identify when I was initially motivated by external factors like socialization, my personal needs and those of my family, and the need to achieve my hopes and ambitions. Even though scientifically, the process of decision-making may seem more apparent, there is an even bigger question that I believe is helpful for understanding the precursors to the decisions we make. As a psychology instructor, there is a study that researchers have debated for years called Nature versus Nurture. It simply attempts to identify the origin of influences that impact human behaviors and mental processes. Nature considers genetic/biological factors while Nurture considers the factors associated with the environment that surrounds us. It is simply the investigation to find out what has a greater impact, heredity, what is passed down from our parents and ancestors or the environment, what structures, culture, and support surround us.

When considering genetics, has someone ever told you that you act or do something like your parent, aunt, or some other relative? It could be the way you look or even some of your mannerisms that become an obvious comparison. My wife says that I walk, talk, and breathe like my biological father. When thinking about it, she's right. I have noticed those similarities as well as others that I have with him. I, like my father, enjoy exploring new places and looking for opportunities that have long-term benefits, like certain careers and investments. Growing up, I didn't live with my biological father. I lived with my stepfather and mother. My stepfather had a calm and relaxed demeanor most of the time. With his even-tempered character, he built positive relationships with those he came in contact with, and as a result, was considered an approachable and trusting person. I have been told by people who knew my mother and biological father that my personality was definitely unique because they were both highly energetic extroverts which is the total opposite of my personality. Because of the impact of my stepfather's presence in my life and the environment he and my mother provided me, I believe that how I engage with others now is significantly influenced by my childhood household experience.

Have you made decisions in a similar manner to the way someone else biologically related does? These examples are Nature oriented. The assumption is that these traits are inherited, so they are passed from one relative to the next.

When considering the concept of Nurture, you learn by observing and engaging in your environment. This environment includes the conditions in which one lives, the values and morals that have been taught, the economic conditions experienced, the people in our lives, the education system, and the era. This is called an ecological model. Think about the environment where you grew up. How did it influence the way you think about life? Of what you have experienced, how does it contribute to the decisions you make today? The movie Twins (1988) starring Danny Davito and Arnold Swarzenegger is a great and funny example of the concept of Nature versus Nurture.

They were twins separated at birth in two totally different environments thousands of miles apart. One twin grew up in an environment of lack, threats, and had to learn urban survival skills while the other twin was raised in an environment with no personal threats and all of his personal and academic needs satisfied. Though the two were miles apart and had different life experiences, they reunited as adults and recognized they had similar mannerisms and excelled in the skills of the environment they were taught.

Many researchers believe it is the interaction between genetics and our environment that contributes to our behavioral characteristics. Psychologist and Stanford University professor Phillip Zimbardo (2001) stated that we all have the genetic potential in us but it is the environment that brings the potential out. In other words, in every human, genes exist that are composed of the material needed to produce an action or expression that has been passed down through heredity but it is the environment that activates the material to release them. So now, I will discuss the impact of influence on our decision-making.

Oxford Dictionary on Lexico.com defines influence as *the capacity to have an effect on the character, development, or behavior of someone or something, or the effect itself.* Think about what had an effect on your character, physical or spiritual development, and behaviors. For many years, I attended a Christian church in Georgia. For me, church was like going to school. I learned how to live a Christ-centered practical life that honored God. In one service that I attended, the senior pastor explained the process of how people arrive where they are in life. It is an eight-point process that helped me understand why I thought the way I thought and why I did the things I have done. The book 8 Steps to Create the Life You Want, The Anatomy of a Successful Life, Dr. Creflo Dollar explained the impact of influence has on our life.

To summarize what I learned, here are the eight steps: 1) There is a Source of Information that influences our thoughts. 2) Thoughts contribute to how we feel. 3) Feelings of the thoughts we have influence our 4) Decisions. The decisions we make lead to the 5)

Actions of how we will respond. Actions lead to 6) Habits based on the decisions we make and the feelings we had about something. Our habits contribute to our 7) Character which is in response to our actions from the decisions we make that are based on the feelings and thoughts of what we understand from our source of information. The final response to the steps is 8) Destination. Destination is the result of the previous seven steps which was influenced by a way of thinking.

This impacted me by giving me an opportunity to examine my motives from where they originated. To continue with what I learned from the message, I was able to understand that the source of any influence and our attitudes towards it is the beginning of the decision-making process. "Why don't I like to be the first in class to raise my hand?" "Why do I hesitate to respond when similar situations occur?" "Why do I feel the need to eat all the food off my plate or make sure all the toothpaste is gone before I get a new tube?" "Why am I more vocal in certain conversations than others?" These types of questions all can be answered and understood if we identify how we initially engaged with the source of our influence.

Here's a simple example of the impact of influence. A student was told by someone she trusts to always be the first person in the class to complete and turn in tests when they are administered.

To illustrate the eight steps using this example above, Step 1) Influence - The student received information that it is good to finish tests first from someone she trusts (the source of influence). Step 2) Thought - The student considers that the information she receives has some sort of validity because she trusts the source. Step 3) Feelings - The student believes what the trusted person shared with her is advantageous and beneficial, as a result, feels comfortable and confident with the information. Step 4) Decision - The student decides to be the first person to complete and turn in her tests. 5) Actions - When the student takes a test, she makes it her effort to be the first to complete it and turn it in. 6) Habits - The student strives to be the first to complete and turn in her tests all the time. 7) Character - The student repeats the behavior of completing tests first and becomes an expected behavior from her. 8) Destination - The consequences of the student's decision to be the first may have positive or negative outcomes. The desire to be first does not mean that she passed the tests, it just means that she turns her test in first.

If you think about the example, it all began with an influence to do something. The source of influence may have all the validity to back the information shared; however, that same source may have had information shared by his or her source of influence in a different era or with contextual differences. That information may not have been researched and biased. It is quite possible that the reason for the student to finish her tests first is not applicable or out of context for her present situation. This example should begin to encourage you to think about the origins of your habits, character, and ultimately your current position in life. The way to do that is to consider your current position and reverse the eight-step process. This will bring you back to the source where the process began.

Understanding why we think and act the way we do grants us an opportunity to evaluate our lives to identify our strengths and areas we need to improve. What motivates you to be strong in the areas you excel? Is it something you observed and admire someone else did successfully? Could it be that you saw a weakness in a parent that upset you, so you made a decision to be strong in the area where the parent was not?

While searching Google for a formal definition for the word "decision," it listed it as: a conclusion or resolution reached after consideration; the action or process of deciding something or of resolving a question; a formal judgment. In the definition, the words conclusion, resolution, and judgment are prominent. The process of getting to any of these endpoints suggests that there must be consideration of the variables and factors we confront. Think of the decisions we all make when we choose the people we decide to embrace as friends. What are the characteristics that have helped you conclude, resolve, or judge these people to qualify as your friends? I chose the friend example because we do not allow just random people in our lives to be friends. Likewise, we need to be just as intentional with the choices we make by thinking of, not just the immediate but also the future desired outcomes.

CHAPTER 5:
INTENTIONAL MOTIVATIONS

One of my favorite movie series to watch is Rocky. After watching them, I feel like doing an intense workout and conquering my toughest goal. After all, the theme of Rocky movies illustrates the process of starting from a point of disadvantage and developing into a top-notch contender. In the Rocky spin-off, Creed, the lead character, Adonis Johnson, the illegitimate son of the deceased Apollo Creed, Rocky's former opponent and later, trainer and friend, was moving up the success ladder early in his work career. He loved the sport of boxing. While in the process of building a career outside the ring, he took excursions out of the country to fight in Mexico. There was something in him that compelled him to see how good he could be in the sport. He knew that his father was a great champion, but without having any knowledge of who his father was until his pre-teenage years, thus having no relationship with him for support and identity, he decided to resign from his job and become a full-time boxer against the wishes of his adoptive mother and initially Rocky.

Adonis made a decision that was not motivated by money or to fight his way to a title. In fact, he had money, a budding career, and a supportive mother. Adonis' decision was based on a desire to identify his potential to be a great fighter. He loved the sport and showed talent in it but had no clue on how far he could take it. He realized a career outside of boxing would result in him not feeling self-fulfilled. This would be called Self-Actualization according to Maslow's Hierarchy of Needs. The movie chronicles Adonis' journey to self-fulfillment. It is also an illustration of Survival, Love and Belonging, Power, Freedom, and Fun, the five core concepts of Glasser's Choice Theory. To make a path in his life based on personal interests that motivated him to sacrifice the available resources he had for an opportunity to pursue a path that he experienced and defined. It was his desire to pursue his self-identity that influenced him to make his choice.

So for Adonis, it was self-identity. The decision he made included the obstacles and challenges that came along with it. It was the motivation to discover his self-identity that was the catalyst for his actions, which developed into the habits of discipline to achieve his goal, formed his character, and ultimately led him to achieve what he desired.

Les Brown, a famed motivational speaker, was quoted saying, "You take on the responsibility for making your dreams a reality." What I understand from this quote is that if you want to accomplish something, you have to go after it because nobody else is responsible for fulfilling your desires.

Your decision needs to be intentional. Having an intended purpose precedes the corresponding actions necessary for goal achievement. After graduating from college, I did not have a plan regarding what I wanted to accomplish in life. In my mind, I thought having a college degree would open career doors and all that I would have to do is apply for the job I wanted, show on my resume that I'm a college graduate, and the job would be mine. I thought that my earned degree was all I needed to be successful. For the cost to attend college and attending four more years of school after high school, I figured that success was expected. Was I wrong! Competition for employment was fierce. Another prominent quote from Les Brown is "Wants show up in conversation - Expectations show up in behavior." Anybody can say they want something but a person who expects something demonstrates quality efforts to get what he or she wants. If I had a specific focus for what I really wanted to do in my life when I was in college, my behaviors in college would have been more intentional and aimed towards my goal rather than just wanting to earn a degree. If I tuned in to quality mentorship with understanding like this in my teens, I would have accomplished so much more.

In college, I had a roommate named Bilal. From the first time I met him as a freshman, he desired to become a dentist and majored in Biology. Bilal enjoyed college life to the fullest. He participated in the Biology Club, he was a member of his state's pre-alumni organization, modeled, was in mentorship and greek-letter organizations, and was also very social on campus. When I mean social, he enjoyed going to parties and hanging out as often as possible. At times, his activities interfered with his grades on assignments and tests. The demanding schedule as a Biology major required much of his attention to study. There were times when he made decisions to not participate in activities or events so he can study and complete projects. His participation in his activities had to be prioritized to not interfere with what it took for him to successfully pass his courses. I can tell you, there were times when it was hard for Bilal to create a good balance. He was stressed many times because of his commitments to various organizations, his desires to be social, times when he needed money, fulfilling family expectations, and finding time to study to make the grades he needed to make.

Bilal's determination and commitment eventually paid off. He is now a successful dentist with his own practice. What was the motivation that pushed him to press through the challenges he encountered? Could it have been the prestige of becoming a successful dentist? Could it have been a commitment to help support his family? Perhaps, he knew a dentist he respected that he wanted to model. Regardless of what it was, it was an influence that was powerful enough for him to make the decisions that got him to his current destination.

Eric Thomas, a famed motivational speaker, was quoted saying, "Don't make a habit out of choosing what feels good over what's actually good for you." It is easy to gravitate towards behaviors that make us feel comfortable but that comfort usually does not contribute to what is going to help us be better. In the context of this book, this quote means to not make decisions based solely on your comfort level. There will be decisions needed to be made where the resulting benefits are better than choosing the less confrontational path.

CHAPTER 6:
PROGRAMMING YOUR
DECISION-MAKING

In the book of Proverbs (The Passion Translation) there is a scripture that says *You can rationalize it all you want and justify the path of error you have chosen, but you'll find out in the end that you took the road to destruction.* Some decisions we make may seem right but may be detrimental to ourselves and others around us. Making decisions out of habit, impulse, or by negative influences will lead you to a destination that you don't see coming. We rationalize poor choices by limiting them to statements like, *"I always do it this way"* or *"This is how I was taught."* We may also say *"I saw someone do it and it worked."* Not all decisions that stem from statements like these are poor; however, when we don't consider the factors that are involved in our decision-making, we may implement an antiquated way of thinking, the Old Map, that no longer benefits the purpose for how we make choices.

Here's an example I heard that demonstrates the old map. It is a story of a wife preparing to roast a ham while being observed by her husband. The wife cut the ends off the ham on each side after preparing it and then placed it in a pan. The husband asked the wife why she cut the ends from the ham? The wife replied, "My mom does it this way so I learned from her." The husband then asked her why did her mother cut the ends off the ham? The wife replied, "I don't know why she cut the ends off." She decided to call her mom and ask why. Her mom told her that she learned to prepare a ham the same way her mother did. The wife was curious as to why her grandmother cut the ends off the ham. Her grandmother was deceased but her grandfather was alive. She called her grandfather to find out why her grandmother cut the ends of the ham off. Her grandfather thought for a moment to remember and then told her. He said, "Your grandmother cut the ends of the ham off because the pan she used to cook it was too small to fit the whole ham." The theme of the story illustrates how learned behaviors and habits may lead to missed opportunities or deficits. In this example, both the wife and her mother cut off the ends of their ham without even knowing why they did it. There was nothing wrong with the ends of the ham, they just got rid of them.

I remember a time when my wife, Rhoda, and I had some of her family over for breakfast early in our marriage. She made eggs, bacon, toast, and grits. Everything looked good on the table and even better as it was arranged on my plate. I took a taste of the eggs and bacon and they were cooked and prepared to perfection. Then I tasted the grits. Now for me, I was used to having my grits made with salt, pepper, butter, and sometimes cheese. When I tasted the grits that she took her precious time to prepare, it tasted sweet. I asked Rhoda why she made the grits with sugar? She said she put sugar in the grits because her mom put sugar in a lot of the foods she prepared when she was growing up. In fact, the reason her mom put sugar in the foods she prepared was because she wanted to make sure that her kids liked the taste of the food she prepared to make sure that food wouldn't go to waste. She did that because money was tight with seven kids to support. Rhoda thought by making sweet grits everyone would like it. My reason for not making grits sweet is because my mom never prepared it with sugar for me, therefore, it wasn't introduced to me. There is nothing wrong with preparing grits either way but in certain situations, to get the best result, considering how to prepare it in a way that it could be enjoyed by everyone that eats grits would have a better outcome. This could be done by having sugar on the table for people who want it and not mixed in the big pot of grits.

There are prescribed patterns that exist that produce an outcome like a boxed cake recipe, if we follow the instructions, we create a cake like the image we see on the box. The question we need to ask ourselves is, "Are we getting the results we want by what we're doing or are we going through the motions because of habit?"

CHALLENGE QUESTIONS

1) Was there ever a time when you realized the way you think and do things were similar to someone you spent significant time with?

2) What are the current habits that you learned from someone you live (d) with in your household?

3) If it's necessary to make a change in your long-time habits, how would you go about making the adjustment?

4) What are some prior habits that have changed as a result of your goals?

CHAPTER 7:
THE POWER OF YOUR MINDSET

In my favorite book for instruction and inspiration, here are two scriptures that discuss mindset. The first, *Whatever is noble, whatever is right, whatever is pure, whatever is lovely, whatever is admirable-if anything is excellent or praiseworthy-think about such things.* The second is, *As someone thinks within himself, so he is.*

These passages assert that what we are or will become is a result of what and how we think and feel about ourselves. In the context of decision-making, the way we think and feel about our choices has an impact on the outcome of our decisions. Keep in mind the many sources of influences that impact our lives.

What have we linked ourselves to that has formed chains that hold us to the foundations of our thoughts regarding various aspects of our lives from the choices we make? Has someone ever told you that you're not a leader? Even if nobody did, how would it make you feel to hear someone else's thoughts about you?

Les Brown shared a story about a time when he was asked by a teacher, Mr. Washington, when he was a student in school to write something on the board. He told Mr. Washington that he couldn't do it because he was labeled by the school as educable mentally retarded. Les had been labeled this from an early age after getting left back in school twice and not having the successful academic achievement like that of his twin brother, Wesley. Mr. Washington wasn't aware of Les' diagnosis and he really didn't care about it. He told him, "Mr. Brown, don't let someone's opinion of you become your reality." Until this point in Les' life, he accepted the label placed upon him and his performance reflected it. A mentoring relationship was formed between him and Mr. Washington that challenged his negative way of thinking about himself into one that increased his confidence over time. This is an example of the power of influence and its effect on a person's mindset. Les decided to change the way he thought about himself which naturally changed the way he felt about himself, leading to decisions, actions, and habits that contributed to the person he became. Les Brown went on to become a top radio disc jockey, a member of Ohio's state congress, best selling author, talk show host, and a leader in the speaking industry.

Famed champion football coach in the late 1950s through 1960s, Vince Lombardi, said, "Leaders are made, they are not born. They are made by hard effort, which is the price all of us must pay to achieve any goal that is worthwhile." Sometimes making decisions can be difficult especially when a choice has to be made that affects others. Just as Vince Lombardi said about leaders, good decision-making can be developed also. Taking initiative, making choices that stretch our comfort zone, and thinking about how benefits outweigh consequences are strategies to use in the practice of making good choices. The practice of quality thinking and then choosing facilitates confidence when positive results occur more frequently than not. Even when not making the best decisions, you can learn from them and make better decisions the next time by considering what factors would produce the outcome better. The practice of great decision-making develops in correlation with a person's self-confidence when choosing.

CHAPTER 8:
INDECISION

There are times when making a choice is so difficult we get stuck. Getting stuck is not unusual but not getting unstuck is a problem. This is called indecision. Another word for indecision is irresolute. Merriam-Webster.com defined irresolute as uncertain how to act or proceed: vacillating. Uncertainty and vacillating are associated with fear. Dr. Dale Dwyer Ph.D. wrote an article in PsychologyToday.com (2019) The Challenge of Indecision, said, "people allow fears to paralyze us to the point that we cannot decide anything." Dr. Dwyer went on to say that because of a lack of confidence which results in indecisiveness because of fear, people are "forced to make a decision, whether it is the one we want to or not." This allows the circumstances or others to *"dictate our decisions, rather than depending upon our inner voice to help us."* He also discussed three symptoms associated with the fear of outcomes when making a decision.

The symptoms are Procrastination, Optimal Choice, and Missed Information.

Here is an excerpt from the article regarding procrastination.

> We procrastinate when we fear a threat to our sense of worth and independence. We only act lazy when our natural drive for fruitful activity is threatened or suppressed. The deep inner fears that cause us to seek such unproductive forms of relief are suggested to be the fear of failure, the fear of being imperfect, _perfectionism_, and the fear of impossible expectations, of being overwhelmed. These fears prevent us from working on and attaining possible _goals_ and relationships. [2]

> Procrastination is a means of escape from reality. The person who procrastinates is like the person who avoids conflict, i.e., "If I don't deal with the issue or problem, it will go away." But rarely does a problem just disappear, particularly problems that real people and real organizations face. More often than not, problems increase in scope, depth, or impact as time passes and we put off the decision.

Symptom Two of indecision is Optimal Choice. Optimal Choice occurs when we "overvalue the importance of the outcome of a decision and react by vacillating between choices." When a person does this, he or she carefully reviews in detail the possible outcomes of every choice to find the best outcome. The issue is getting stuck looking for the best option for fear of making a poor decision. Finally, there's Symptom Three, Missing Information, the issue of becoming overwhelmed with so much information an individual gathers to make the best choice to avoid missing any detail that the person gets stuck. It's just too much information to choose from.

Fear is the underlying issue for all the symptoms of indecision described by Dr. Dwyer. Denzel Washington, an academy award-winning actor said, "You pray for rain, you gotta deal with the mud too. That's part of it." In the context of decision-making, this quote conveys, with the opportunity of making a good choice, there's also the possibility of unexpected and undesired consequences. You have to decide and act on it and not allow fear of consequences to hinder you.

Fear is defined as a distressing emotion aroused by impending danger, evil, pain, whether the threat is real or imagined, the feeling or condition of being afraid. (www.Dictionary.com. 2020) As indecision is an expression of fear, so is anger and self-centeredness. Both of these expressions have an effect on decision-making. Fear is an uncomfortable feeling for people because it makes them feel vulnerable and not in control of a situation. To avoid feeling this way, people shift from feeling vulnerable to anger because anger makes a person feel more in charge and less helpless.

(Healthpsych.com, Pratt. 2014) When making decisions angrily, a person's focus is distracted between their emotions and objectively making a choice.

Self-Centeredness, as an expression of fear, is associated with self-worth and consists of two factors: 1) Lacking a sense of self, our authentic identity, and 2) Projecting our fear of unworthiness to others (Rose, 2019). When we're preoccupied with our own negative "self-talk" that we perceive others may be thinking about our ability to make the right choice, we make decisions based on what we believe others want us to make rather than what we may consider to be the best decision.

CHALLENGE QUESTIONS

1) What kinds of fears have prevented you from making major decisions?

2) What were the situations that led to indecision when you had to make a significant decision?

3) Thinking back when you had to make a major decision but experienced indecision, how did you feel about yourself? Were you able to finally make a decision? If so, how?

4) What were some influences that contributed to the way you felt about yourself at that time?

5) How often do you feel this way when making decisions?

CHAPTER 9:
DECISION-MAKING STRATEGIES

Because making choices in life is inevitable for all humans and not every decision is simple to make, strategies for making better decisions have been developed to help. In 2020, Jayson Demers wrote an article in Inc.com called *7 Strategies for Making Objective Decisions* that identified tips to help with the process. The strategies are: 1) Acknowledge and Compensate Your Biases, 2) Use Pro and Con Lists, 3) Imagine Counseling a Friend, 4) Strip Down Your Deciding Factors, 5) Experiment By Reversing Your Line of Thinking, 6) Create a Scoring System, and 7) Make a Decision and Live With It.

When acknowledging and compensating your biases, people should think critically about what reduces objective decision-making; decisions based on information directly related to its effect on the outcome. Past experiences, assumptions towards the choices, and our characteristic attitudes contribute to biased and subjective decision-making. It was advised in the article to think about these factors carefully and lean toward or away from an option because of these biases to restructure our thinking.

Creating a Pro and Con list is a way to help make a better decision by writing down a list of the benefits of an option and another list for anything negative an option may have. In addition to writing a list of positives and negatives factors, it's helpful to scale the importance of each factor to help identify the best options.

Visualizing yourself counseling a friend regarding a decision that needs to be made can "help you understand what an outsider's perspective might be." This strategy is designed to reduce distortions because of existing personal biases and focus on the most important information provided by your friend who has to make the same choice. As a counselor, you are able to identify objective details clearer than a client would because a counselor must separate his or her biases when counseling a client to provide quality assistance.

Stripping down deciding factors is a strategy that eliminates any factor that isn't a primary consideration for a decision. The idea is to reduce factors to ones that are most important to keep deciding factors to a minimum. This helps to eliminate biases that make decision making more challenging.

Reversing your line of thinking is a strategy that proposes that we all make assumptions when we make decisions. It suggests that you consider the possibility of what may happen if the opposite of your assumption is the outcome. How likely would you make that same choice?

Creating a scoring system is a tip that suggests you assign positive and negative points of worth to factors surrounding your decision. Once all factors are considered and the points are tabulated, one decision will objectively be worth more than the other.

The final strategy is to decide and live with it. The idea of this strategy is that it's better to make a decision rather than not to make one. Even if your decision doesn't result in the outcome you expected, you will handle the issues when they come anyway. Making a poor decision will be a learning experience for a similar decision in the future.

Jennifer Verdolin Ph.D. (2018) shared three strategies for better decision-making. She suggested that we should first gather as much information regarding our choices to help us make the best choice possible. Second, impulsive decisions are usually made when you're under stress. It's necessary to recognize your internal state, your emotions. If you're stressed, take some time and do things to reduce stress. The time you take will help minimize making a poor decision. The third strategy is to pursue incremental improvements. Dr. Verdolin said it's not necessary to wait for the best decision. Exploring your range of options in addition to exploring new situations can help with updating the information we have towards making decisions.

In addition to these strategies, it's important that we have confidence that we are capable of making a good decision. The strategies previously discussed share practical examples of what can be done to make better decisions, but it's the confidence facilitated by positive influences that impact our lives to attract the best strategies for making better choices. There is a proverb that says, *As a man thinketh in his heart, so is he.* When we believe we are capable of making good decisions, we gain confidence and make better decisions because we have eliminated the negative biases ushered by doubt that complicate the decision-making process. Henry Ford, with only eight years of education in a one-room school, revolutionized the personal transportation industry and founded Ford Motor Company in the early 1900s, said, "If you think you can do a thing or think you can't do a thing, you're right." Making better decisions begins with positive thoughts about your ability to make good choices which will develop confidence. This mindset is the foundation for the law of attraction which asserts that thinking positive or negative brings positive or negative experiences into an individual's life.

CHAPTER 10:
RECOGNIZE THE DIRECTION OF YOUR ATTITUDE

There is an instrument on aircraft that's necessary "to provide the pilot or pilots with an artificial horizon when the true horizon is not visible to them." This instrument is called the Attitude Directional Indicator (ADI) (Graves. Aea.net, 2005). It indicates the orientation of the aircraft so that the pilot can identify if he or she is following the planned coordinates to its destination. It considers the aircraft's atmospheric conditions and position to the ground. If you think about it, if an aircraft's position is one degree off in any direction from its flight plan for 60 nautical miles, it will be off course by one nautical mile. Unless the pilot makes adjustments in flight once he or she sees the deviation from the flight plan, it will not arrive where it is supposed to land.

Whether it's good or bad, we all have an attitude. Dictionary.com defines attitude as *manner, disposition, feeling, position, etc., with regard to a person, or thing; tendency or orientation, especially in the mind.* As shared earlier, the influences in our life affect our attitude that will produce our thoughts and emotions that facilitate our decisions. Like the ADI gauge of an aircraft, our decisions are significantly impacted by our attitude. In addition to our attitudes influenced by others, attitudes are also contextual to specific issues or conditions that are present at the time a decision needs to be made.

When you're sick, emotionally unbalanced, burdened by daily stressors, or other things that may negatively impact your life, if you have to make a decision, it could be impaired. Remember a time you had to make a decision when you were under pressure. Were you able to think clearly without the interference of your stressors in the back of your mind? Stressors are distractors to making better decisions. Stressors in life are inevitable but it's how we handle the stressors that will determine the effectiveness of our decision-making. Checking our attitude before making a decision like a pilot checks the ADI gauge to determine if the aircraft's position is on course to its destination is important. Having a negative attitude before making a decision can set you off course because the focus will not entirely be on the outcome but shared with having to deal with the stressors.

Making mental adjustments to keep you on course where you can refocus will give you the best opportunity to achieve your desired outcome from your choice. These adjustments can be made by holding off the decision until the stressors have been settled or until you are able to separate your emotions tied to the stressors. Refocusing on your source of inspiration, spiritual or physical, is a way to get clarity, grounded, and strengthen your ability to make a sound decision. Remembering your source is the key! The ability to make good decisions is already in us.

Here's an illustration on the topic of potential I learned in graduate school using a potted plant. If a potted plant is provided the right amount of food, water, the ideal temperature and lighting, and the right amount of soil, the plant will grow to its fullest potential. Here's the flip side to this illustration. Though the potential is in the plant for it to grow optimally, if the plant does not get the right amount of water, if the lighting and temperature are inconsistent, and if the soil has been littered with rocks, the plant will grow but its full potential will be hindered by the impact of its conditions. It may grow shorter, bent, twisted, or have a weak foundation. Like the potted plant illustration, our ability to make the best choices may be impaired by our circumstances but if we can learn to effectively manage the battles in our mind, our decision-making abilities will flourish. Managing the battles in our mind can be accomplished by identifying your strengths, acknowledging what isn't in your ability to control, and finding ways to use the strengths to your advantage.

Have you experienced a time when someone brings up a negative habit or past decision you made in your life that impacted him or her? Perhaps you overcame the issue or maybe you're working through the issue but it's not at the pace the person who continues to bring it up expects to see results. It's not an easy position to be in because you know that you made decisions that had a negative impact on his or her life. Once you have accepted the responsibility of those past decisions and continually commit to making a change with your corresponding actions, you're doing your part.

We cannot change the attitude or opinions of someone else about you. We can only change ourselves. Accepting negative opinions that people have towards you impacts you by adding additional stressors to what life already gives you. They won't and don't help you. Understanding that change starts first on the inside, your mindset, like the small rutter at the end of a boat determines what direction it will go, your path will take direction. Your positive mindset is your motivation; your influence towards making better choices. It will provide the condition, like in the example of the potted plant, you will need to grow to be the best version of yourself and be a shield to the distractions that will attempt to take you off course.

CHAPTER 11:
FROM THE BRICKS: THE STORY
OF THE WALLACE BROTHERS

In the late 1970s through 1980s, two young brothers in their early teens, Wilson and Michael Wallace lived in Newark, New Jersey, which was known as the "Brick City" on Spruce Street. Wilson was the older of the two by two years. Common sights in the neighborhood where they lived were properties with no grass, broken glass on the streets, and alleys between graffiti-tagged buildings, drugs, and liquor stores on the corners. Kids played football and jumped double dutch on the cracked asphalt. The basketball courts in the neighborhood had chain nets if any and stained mattresses piled outside of buildings were used as trampolines by the neighborhood kids.

Wilson and Michael lived on the first floor in a two bedroom and one bathroom apartment in an all brick government-assisted four-story building with their sixty-five-year-old grandmother who had custody of them and their older sister due to the untimely death of their young mother. Upon entering the building where they lived was an exterior door that opened to a foyer with a damaged and soiled tile floor leading to an internal staircase with two stoops on each side where residents often sat and watched who came in and out of the building. At the top of the staircase were two heavy metal dented doors, as if they had been kicked, surrounded by steel frames and security glass where people entered the residence halls. The smell of alcohol, urine, and garbage were heavy throughout the building. In addition to the odor that permeated the building, it was common to see rodents and insects scampering at night or their remains located in the places where they died.

The hot water in the buildings seldom worked, so residents would often take cold showers or baths to clean themselves. Sometimes the heat didn't work, so the building residents were cold in the winter. The screens in the windows were torn or missing so in the spring and summer months, residents on the first and second floor could hear clearly what was being said or going on in the streets outside the building. Crimes were frequent and it was rare to see police patrol the neighborhood.

Life was a challenge for the brothers. Their grandmother, who they called mom, had only a second grade education and could barely read. Government assistance, which she used to support her household, was her only source of income. There was no adult male figure in the brothers' life for support or guidance because the brothers only saw their father a handful of unpleasant times.

Wilson and Michael looked different from most of the other kids in the community because their skin was lighter and their hair texture was straighter in comparison to their peers. Acceptance by peers was important for survival in their neighborhood so the brothers had to prove themselves, many times by doing things they didn't agree with, to fit in and establish street credibility. Close family members only saw or heard about the behaviors of what Wilson and Michael did on the streets, so they didn't have any positive or supportive words to say to or about them, only berating comments.

As high school students, the brothers did not take their education seriously. No one in their household taught them the importance of education or had conversations about the future they would like to have. All the brothers saw was what their community presented. They didn't know what they wanted to be in life or what accomplishments they could achieve. Wilson was not interested in going to college after high school because he didn't like school in the first place and would rather make money to look and dress nicely. An army recruiter visited his high school to talk to the students about the opportunities that would be available if they join. At that time, Wilson didn't give a thought about joining the military much attention.

Earlier, when Wilson was in middle school, he went on a tour that made an impression on his life. It was a trip to a manufacturing building where he saw people that looked and dressed the way he desired with nice shirts, slacks, shoes, and name badges attached to their waist. Wilson was so intrigued by what he saw that he asked the tour guide what kind of work they did. The tour guide explained that these were call center workers and explained the positions within the organization. Once he found out about what a CEO was, he was intrigued. An adult accompanying him on the tour asked him what he wanted to do for a career. Wilson said jokingly, "I want to be a pharmacist because I can sell drugs legally." Even though he said it to get a laugh out of the other kids on the tour, he enjoyed learning about science. His classmates laughed at his response but the adult paused a moment and responded, "that's a great career choice!" The adult told him that he can do it but he'll need to further his education beyond high school. Wilson knew that he didn't have money to pay for college so he didn't think it was possible for him to become a pharmacist.

Upon graduating high school, he didn't have plans for his future laid out but he knew he wanted something better for himself. He decided to join the military but chose the Navy over the Army because it was a branch that wasn't frequently advertised where he lived. He decided to take the Military Entrance Process Station (MEPS) Exam just to see what score he could earn.

While waiting to take the exam, he saw videos of the various career paths the military could make available to him. He was wowed by what he saw regarding aviation programs. The recruiter saw his interest and found out from his test scores that he qualified for an aviation technician position and signed him into the Navy on delayed entry.

He and a friend were sitting around one day with nothing planned and decided to apply for a job so they can make money. They decided to apply for Macy's-Bambergers, a big department store hiring temporary seasonal workers. He applied and was hired as a clerk but his friend wasn't because he had a criminal record. So Wilson worked and excelled. His performance was acknowledged and he worked as many hours as he could because he was making money, dressed better like the workers he remembered seeing on the junior high school tour, and he felt like he was a part of something good.

When his time as a seasonal employee expired, he realized that he was good at something positive and saw the benefits that resulted from his diligent work. His work was appreciated by his supervisor that he was referred to another department to work full-time where he also excelled and was promoted. He worked until it was time for him to go to basic training in the military.

Wilson's military experience was eye-opening because it exposed him to people of different cultures, new skills, and different countries. Prior to the military, New York and New Jersey were the only states he visited. After completing basic training, he took leave and came back to Newark to check on Michael and to share his military experience.

Michael was a senior in high school going through the motions of life as he knew it. Like Wilson, Mike had no guidance and was barely passing his courses in school. When Wilson visited home on a military leave, he had a conversation with Michael about the benefits of joining the military; the pay, health insurance, and the meals. He also shared with his brother about the countries he visited and let him know that there was a better life outside of Newark. Wilson was experiencing better things and wanted for his brother to have the opportunity as well.

One day Michael was walking home after graduating high school, looked around at his surroundings of his declining community, and knew he needed to make a change. He contacted an Air Force Recruiter who arranged for him to take the MEPS exam at the advice of his brother. He tested into a remedial program. While in the program, he realized people outside of his cultural background didn't know as much as he thought they did. He also realized that the way math was taught in the military was different than in high school. With determination and the assistance of study groups, Michael excelled in his military education and training. While serving in the military, he was intrigued by the soldiers who were engineers. He was even more fascinated with the money they earned. Michael was competitive and believed that he could do anything he saw others do, especially if it would benefit his goal to live a successful and enjoyable life. He had the drive to be better and to do better.

After serving his time in the Air Force, Mike made the decision to go to school to become an engineer. He excelled in mathematics and upon earning his degree and was employed with a major engineering corporation. In addition to becoming an engineer, he became a college math instructor, mentor, earned a real estate broker license, and owns a brokerage firm. As a result of the sincere conversation Wilson shared with Mike about a way to live better, a new world of experiences and opportunities became available that enriched his life.

Wilson credited the military with teaching him the importance of being a responsible and accountable person, characteristics he didn't learn growing up. After serving in the military as an aviation technician, he decided to enroll in school to study science, the subject he was interested in from an early age. Today, Wilson is a Radiologic Technologist with MRI and CT credentials. He shares his story to motivate and inspire youth and young adults to have goals and that it's possible to experience a better life with his story.

Both Wilson and Mike have families of their own and are proud grandparents. The success they achieved after the military was not without personal trials that each experienced, but with support for one another and surrounding themselves with caring people, they were able to persevere to reach the outcomes they are now enjoying. What began as a darkly shaded and unfortunate life experience as youths that could have negatively impacted their future, they were motivated by finding a way to have a better life using a resource that was available to them; the military.

The structure the military provided them taught them how to focus on their objective and as a result, they engaged in activities that contributed to the success they both achieved. As a result of their commitment to make a change in their lives, their children became doctors, lawyers, successful business owners, and leading industry professionals.

CHALLENGE QUESTIONS

1) Who or what were early influences in your life that impacted some of the important decisions you've made?

2) Why were the influences so impactful on your life?

3) What feelings come up when you think about the impact your influence(s) had on your decisions?

4) What habits do you practice today as a result of your influence(s)?

CHAPTER 12:
THE PURSUIT TOWARDS SUCCESS: THE TANISHA H. SHAW STORY

Tanisha H. Shaw is the founder, and publisher of a very successful online publication, Optimal Living Magazine, and Legacy Living Homes magazine. She is also the author of her very own 30 Day Gratitude Faith Journal and the host of the Diamond Life Producers Podcast. For over one decade, she has been sharing stories of hope, inspiration, Godly wisdom, coping with everyday life, staying focused, and spiritually charged for her readers. At an early age, Tanisha had a gift for writing; but, she was more interested in becoming a doctor of internal medicine. Tanisha credits her mother as her influence to pursue a career in medicine.

Tanisha's mother, a single parent, had her at a young age and worked hard as a bank teller to make ends meet. At the tender age of 3, her mother put a toy stethoscope around her neck and told her she was going to be a medical doctor. From that point on, the seed of reaching for more and becoming a medical doctor had been planted. Tanisha always had an inward knowing that she was a very gifted person and special to God. Because her mother had to work a lot, she told Tanisha that God was everywhere and that she never had to fear anything or anyone. God was always there watching her and only one prayer away. From that point on, she always felt very close to God and knew she had a divine purpose in life to fulfill.

Perhaps, Tanisha's bloodline had something to do with her confidence. Her grandmother told her many stories about her lineage, the Higginbothams from Tennessee, her grandmother had cousins who served as judges, professors, artists, dancers, successful entrepreneurs, as well as Joan Higginbotham, Electrical Engineer and former NASA astronaut, who was the third African-American woman to fly on a space mission.

Growing up, things weren't handed to Tanisha. She lived in a one bedroom apartment with her mother and brother for the first 14 years of her life and worked very hard to meet her basic human needs, and to excel in school as she pursued a career in medicine. She believed the choices she made growing up from junior high school through college were a solution to the issues she encountered daily and for what she expected to happen. Every summer, she participated in college science camps and other projects at Seton Hall University, Rutgers University, New Jersey Institute of Technology, and Fairleigh Dickinson

University to learn everything she could because she believed it would be advantageous towards her career goal.

She was very selective with who she chose to hang out with, and started applying for college scholarships at the age of 15, during her lunch breaks in high school. Her efforts paid off and secured her enough money to attend Rutgers University for six years, tuition free. Tanisha was competitive in her actions; however, she competed to enhance her life, rather than comparing herself to others. While she was a junior pursuing a biochemistry degree, Tanisha had an epiphany while she was completing a chemistry lab project. She thought to herself, *"being able to save lives is awesome, but changing lives through the power of my own words makes me whole."* So, on that afternoon, she returned her chemistry lab tools, went to the Dean's office and asked to have her major switched to English and Journalism.

To her friends and family, it was the ultimate shocker; but for Tanisha, it was a great relief, turning a major page for her destiny. Soon after, she started creating a collection of clips via the campus newspaper. She was given permission to start her own column on campus called, RU Talkin'. RU Talkin' was a big hit on campus, as she wrote real stories about student's thoughts about relationships, politics, and life. She eventually graduated from Rutgers University, then immediately accepted an internship with Black Enterprise Magazine, where she learned journalism from leading industry professionals. This experience was the launchpad that ignited Tanisha's desire to publish her own magazines and podcasts. Here's an excerpt from the Winter 2020 issue of Optimal Living Magazine, where she discussed how intentional her choices were, and the discipline she implemented to accomplish her goals.

Our lives are shaped by the choices we make every single day. When I was 5 years old, I looked up at the sky and had my first conversation with God. At the time, I was not pleased with my living conditions, and it made me determined to work hard to create a better life for myself. I simply said, "God this isn't for me. When I grow up I'm going to be somebody great. I am not meant to live in lack." From that point on, I worked hard and made choices based on where I wanted my life to go. If I wanted to get out of poverty, I had to stay away from the wrong crowd, study hard, open myself up to different academic experiences, get my education and not get pregnant before my time. This meant that I had to say "no" to anything or anybody that was going to keep me from living the "diamond" life of my dreams. In spite of it all, we rise, fall, live, and learn. I started Optimal Living Magazine at the point of my own personal recession. Producing Optimal Living has been a source of personal healing, growth, and revelation on many levels. I've shared life-changing principles and stories that have propelled myself and thousands of our precious readers forward, since 2008. Along the way, I realized some things I would do differently financially, in relationships, and in business, if I would have known what I know today. (Optimal-LivingMagazine.com, Winter 2020)

As Tanisha reflected on her life's journey, she mentioned that she simply made decisions that would benefit what she aspired to achieve. She expected to do great things and the sparkle in her eye drew those types of opportunities to her. Keep in mind, there were times she was confronted with enticing opportunities that had the potential to derail her life. In those instances, she had to pivot. However, at the end of the day, growing up in poverty pushed her to be her very best.

Her inner catalyst was that she was not pleased with the living conditions she experienced as a child growing up, and she had a pet peeve for wasting time. Yet, she came to realize that while in pursuit of your purpose, time is on your side, when you serve the author of time. Therefore, through life's ups and downs, she continues to invest time in her own personal development, her God, her family, and her gifts, in her personal pursuit of a successful life. When life got rough, she remained prayerful, grew in wisdom from her mistakes, adjusted her mindset when necessary, and discovered successful coping tools as she kept committing herself to her goals. Pursuits aren't easy. It requires a chasing action to achieve something you truly desire.

CHALLENGE QUESTIONS

1) What goals are you pursuing?

2) Why are you pursuing the goal(s)?

3) What challenges have you faced in your pursuit?

4) What sacrifices have you made in your pursuit?

5) What have you learned about yourself during your pursuit?

CHAPTER 13:
PUTTING IT ALL TOGETHER

It's inevitable that in our lifetime, we'll make decisions both good and bad. It's a part of all our lives' experience where we have an opportunity to learn and grow from the process as well as the outcomes of the choices we'll make. We all learn and process information uniquely; after all, we're human and not robots. The information passed down genetically from our ancestors, the communities where we dwell, and the culture we identify shaped our mindsets beginning from infancy. They help us when we encounter choices. That information programmed us to engage, retreat, proceed with caution, align, or to reconsider whatever needs a decision from us.

We all have taken in information both pleasant and unpleasant, whether it be something that happened to us personally or something we observed happening to someone else. We've responded to our experiences based on what we determined will have better outcomes. That determination was based on the collection of information acquired and considered which helped us to decide on the course of action that yielded what we felt was the best outcome. Our feelings and attitudes were tied to our choices because of the value we placed on who or what influenced us.

As with the Wallace brothers, who knew they wanted more than what their childhood community presented, motivated to act by the desire to change for a better life, took a chance with their lives and decided it was possible for them to have more and better themselves. The image Wilson saw of himself dressing nicely and working in a clean work environment took root within him. He saw the outcome he wanted for himself. Michael saw that if he took time to invest in learning anything he put his energy towards, he knew that he could compete with his fellow airman because he realized that he could outwork the best of them.

Tanisha's vision of whom she was and where she was heading gave her the strength to endure challenges while staying focused on her prize; becoming a successful businesswoman. She took life's lemons and turned them into lemonade employing grit and determination to follow through on her decision to separate herself from the distractions of lack, fear, and temptations that were in her path.

As you now understand, the process of decision-making isn't automatic. Careful consideration, understanding the source of your motivation for your choices, your emotions at the time of making a decision, and the belief in the outcome are contributing factors. To help make better decisions, which we're all capable of doing, don't just evaluate the situation; evaluate yourself to make sure that your biases aren't in control. Make sure you have a positive attitude about your ability to make a good decision. Lastly, don't allow fear to hinder you from making a decision. Remember, you may not always make the best decisions but it's important to make the decision anyway. The more carefully thought-out the decisions you make, the more you build up your confidence while decreasing indecisiveness.

So in conclusion, when considering every facet that contributes to the efforts for making good choices, Vincent Van Gogh said, "Great things are done by a series of small things brought together." Whether it's choosing your friends, your career choice, your desired lifestyle, your political affiliation, your spirituality, or even the way you think about yourself, a decision is being made and you're the pilot. You must direct your thoughts, feelings, and efforts towards the big picture for your decisions which is the desired outcome. Control the process like a pilot flying to a destination. Now anchor yourself to this truth, the ability to make good choices regardless of the significance begins with your belief that you can do it. That's power, the authority to get results. So when faced with your next decision, big or small; "make your next move a power move."

EQUIPMENT

By

Edgar A. Guest

Figure it out for yourself, lad
You've all that the greatest of men have had,
Two arms, two hands, two legs, two eyes,
And a brain to use if you would be wise,
With this equipment, they all began,
So start for the top and say "I can."

Look them over, the wise and great,
They take their food from a common plate,
And similar knives and forks they use,
With similar laces, they tie their shoes,
The world considers them brave and smart,
But you've all they had when they made their
start.

You can triumph and come to skill,
You can be great if you only will.
You're well equipped for what fight you choose,
You have legs and arms and a brain to use,
And the one who has risen great deeds to do,
Began their life with no more than you.

You are the handicap you must face,
You are the one who must choose your place,

You must say where you want to go,
How much you will study the truth to know.
God has equipped you for life, but He
Lets you decide what you want to be,

Courage must come from the soul within,
You must furnish the will to win.
So figure it out for yourself, my lad,
You were born with all that the great have had,
With your equipment, they all began.
Get hold of yourself, and say: "I can!"

REFERENCES

Cherry, Kendra (2019) Nature Vs Nurture: Genes or Environment. Retrieved from https://www.explorepsychology.com/nature-vs-nurture/

Demers, Jayson (2015). *7 Strategies for Making Objective Decisions.* Retrieved from https://www.inc.com/jayson-demers/7-strategies-for-making-objective-decisions.html

www.Dictionary.com (2020)

Dollar, Creflo (2008). *8 Steps to Create the Life You Want: The Anatomy of a Successful Life* New York, NY: Faithwords

Dwyer, Dale (2019). *The Challenge of Indecision. Why do people suffer from decidophobia?* Retrieved from https://www.psychologytoday.com/us/blog/got-minute/201904/the-challenge-indecision

Glasser Institute for Choice Theory. *Basic Needs.* Retrieved from

https://wglasser.com/what-is-choice-theory/

Graves, Ralph (2005). *ADI. Attitude Directional Indicator.* Retrieved from http://aea.net/AvionicsNews/ANArchives/ADISept05.pdf

www.lexico.com (2020) *Oxford Dictionary*

Learning Theories. *Social Learning Theory.* Retrieved from https://www.learning-theories.com/social-learning-theory-bandura.html

Reitman, Ivan (1988). Twins, Motion Picture, USA, Universal Pictures

Rose, Hanna (2019). *Self-Centered Fear. How to stop thinking that everyone is thinking about you.* Retrieved from https://www.psychologytoday.com/us/blog/working-through-shame/201906/self-centered-fear

Simply Psychology. *Maslow's Hierarchy of Needs.* Retrieved from https://www.simplypsychology.org/maslow.html

Verdolin, Jennifer (2018). *3 Strategies for Better Decision-Making. What to do when indecision strikes.* Retrieved from https://www.psychologytoday.com/us/blog/wild-connections/201807/3-strategies-better-decision-making

Zimbardo, Phillip (2001). *Discovering Psychology: Updated Edition*, WGBH Educational Foundation. https://www.learner.org/series/discovering-psychology

JOE KENLEY WORLDWIDE, LLC.

We believe the information you received from this product has provided you value, so be on the lookout for more from Joe Kenley.

To receive the latest information about upcoming books, projects, or upcoming promotions from Joe Kenley Worldwide, LLC, join our mailing list. Visit kenleyspeaks.org and sign up now!

If you're interested in Joe Kenley speaking to your group or organization in person or virtually, please contact joe@kenleyspeaks.org or request information from our website at www.kenleyspeaks.org.